All Offense.
Always Aggressive.
The Armor of God

by

Andrew Brattrud

TABLE OF CONTENTS

Introduction

My good friend Sefu Steve Garcia and I have a combined MMA record of 56-0. Undefeated! He is 55-0 and I am 1-0. His art, American Kenpo, is brutal. Everything is a weapon. Every weakness is a target. There is only victory. Even when facing paralysis and a long hospital stay, he imagined a form (a series of moves that can be practiced) of fighting from his bed. Over and over, his mind rehearsed. Limited mobility. Pain. But over and over he practiced. A few nights later, one of his hospital roommates snuck out, got drunk and stumbled into his bed. In an instant, he woke up. Calm, calculated and already in motion. Crash! Bang! Boom! The form worked to a "T." His mind only sees a defense that leads to an offense. It only sees his opponent unconscious.

My karate has equipped me. It has taught me that if you have an "empty hand," everything can become a weapon. My instructor once asked about what "karate" was. "If a man attacked me in the parking lot with a knife, and I escaped into my truck then ran him over with my truck, is that karate?" The answer is yes.

The armor of God is fit for Kingdom soldiers. "The Kingdom of God suffers violence and violent men take it by force," Jesus taught. When I echoed that verse in my office, a visitor interrupted, saying "I don't like that. I don't think the Bible would teach that!" Without thinking, I smiled. "It does not matter what you think. The Bible says what it says. How about I replace 'violence' with 'aggression?'" She did not like that either. But it is true.

Every piece of the Ephesians 6 armor is offensive. I have heard it often preached that "only the Sword of the Spirit is for attacking." Negative. Where I am from, we fight tooth and nail. We headbutt with the helmet of salvation. We bear hug with the breastplate of righteousness. We trample and stomp with the boots of the gospel. Our belt is girded, but ready to be a whip. With the shield we press, we press and we press forward. And with the Sword of the Spirit, we swing better than Peter, who only nicked ears.

As "a good soldier does not entangle himself in the affairs of this life so he may please the one who enlisted him," so we Christians focus on the calling God has for us. There is a war. Souls are at stake. Eternal judgment is at stake. Every human being's life is a battlefield for the glory. Jesus came to "destroy the works of the devil." We "tear down strongholds." How? By putting on the armor of God. This book will teach you how, as well as give you examples of great Bible saints. God sent His son. He initiated. He attacked. Jesus cast out devils. He attacked. Shock and Awe. Diseases disappeared. A new domain has come to mankind. There is a new Lord. Jesus showed His power, authority and right to rule. He was aggressive, attacking and armored. Now we are called to "walk as He walked."

RCA

4075 Twining St. Riverside, Ca 92509

Belt of Truth

"Stand firm, girded with the belt of truth."

How is a belt an offensive weapon?" The only people who can ask that are people who never got whooped or spankings. Before the Millennials, no one would question that thought.

The belt of truth shows you are ready. It extends your range. A belt is always with you...so ought to be the truth.

Twice, General Joab was replaced as commander of King David's army. Both Abner and Amasa, who took his job, did not last long. Joab shanked both of them. When he saw each of them, he had his belt on with his dagger loose—they didn't.

The phrase "gird up your loins" is used many times in the Bible. "Stay ready." We learn the truth. It rings differently. We pursue it. It is top of mind. Truth is our mind's meditation. No more lying to ourselves. No more "white lies." That won't allow us to move as we should.

Belts keep you together. They are not always comfortable. The man in the suit has a belt, the officer has a belt, and important days require that you be well put together. It can be uncomfortable...so can the truth. How much do you weigh? Exactly, how much? How much do you spend of things you don't need? Exactly how much? Tell the truth.

If you look up "self-defense" videos on YouTube, the first page will likely have "experts" using their belts. It adds a few feet to the strike. Jesus made a belt-like whip. Tossing tables and cracking, He drove out the moneychangers. When we speak the truth, it goes farther than we think. Offense echoes. Immoral minds will erupt in complaints. They will treat the truth like bad propaganda.

Breastplate

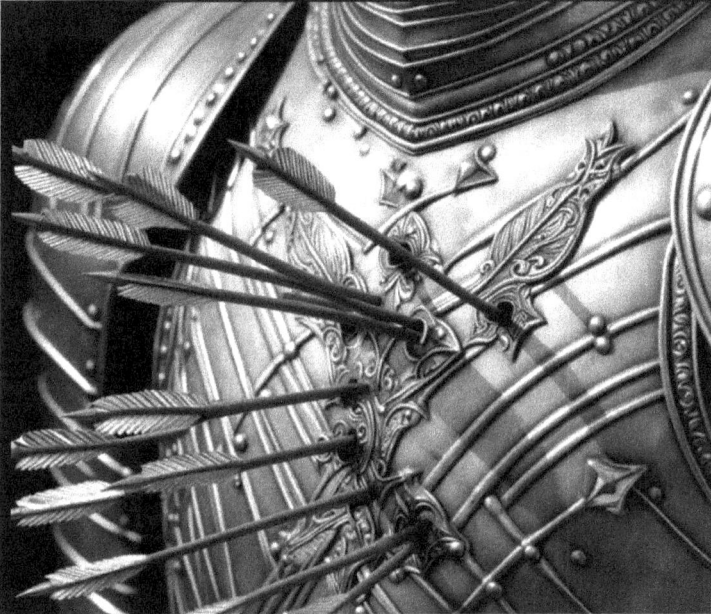

There is a bear hug that breaks the opponent's balance. The hands are locked directly onto the lower spine. Such pressure is extended that it is like a knee-jerk reaction. The legs automatically bend, the body falls and the aggressor takes the advantage. Imagine that move with a bronze breastplate...ouch! Even armor is offensive.

"Stand, having the breastplate of righteousness." What protects your heart? Does it fit? Who is in your heart? God has given us a way to stay right.

King Ahab was warned. The prophet announced "If you go to battle, you will die there." Precautions were taken. He dressed like an ordinary soldier and wore extra-padded armor. But God sees through clever customs. It was a "random arrow" that pierced the plate and gauged him. Slowly, sadly, his life drained as he watched his army defeated, propped up in his chariot.

King Ahab's son also had armor on when he was killed. Jehu was too strong with the bow. It blew by the armor, through the chest and out the other side.

It is the "breastplate of righteousness." Why "righteousness?" To be "righteous" is to be in a right relationship. It is to be declared innocent. How are your relationships? Are they protected? They sure affect your life. In right standing with your family and friends, God gives you courage.

Years ago, I went on a ride along with the Orange County Sheriffs. It was awesome. They are brave. It was the last Friday of the month when the courthouse closes to make all the bailiffs available to serve warrants. As we approached the first apartment to make arrests, they handed me a bulletproof vest. Awesome! "Ok, now I am safe, but do I get a gun too?" They laughed, but I felt safe.

Give a kid a life-vest and they will jump off the diving board! It gives security. Contrast that with the man whose spouse cheated on him. He will be guarded, slow to trust, and will hesitate to show his heart.

The shepherd boy David refused King Saul's armor when going to battle with Goliath. Why? It did not fit. It was not his. He was not used to it. God has a custom plate for you. David could not fight with Saul's armor. I cannot fight with your armor, nor you with mine. What gives you security will not do the same thing for me.

In my heart, I am many things: a father, a husband, a pastor, a coach, a friend, a sensei. Each of these are made by the relationships I have with others. If my heart is right, those relationships can be protected.

The Egyptians had lots of armor. They tried to cross the Red Sea following hard after Moses. It was what they thought would keep them safe that caused them to drown. Wrong armor. Not everything that makes you "feel" secure makes you secure. Sometimes it weighs you down. This is like sinful addictions that offer momentary relief. They are from "spiritual Egypt" the place of bondage.

The great UFC Champion Georges "Rush" St. Pierre had a tattoo over his heart. It is prominent in each of his fights. It looks a bit like the patches martial artists wear on their uniforms, but his never comes off. What never leaves your heart? Better yet, *who* never leaves your heart? The high priest of ancient Israel wore a breastplate that had special stones with each of the names of the Ten Tribes inscribed on them. They were to serve them, pray for them and keep them close.

Christ is to be in our hearts. Our fellow brothers and sisters are to have a place there. Are those relationships protected? Remember, it's always easier to destroy than to build. Whenever you face a situation in relationships with family, friends, or your fellow brothers and sisters, ask yourself: "Am I building or destroying?" When you build, fight for what you have built; protect what you have built.

October 14, 1912, in Milwaukee Wisconsin, Theodore Roosevelt was giving a campaign speech. From the crowd, stretched the arm of a would-be assassin, John Schrank. His .38 Colt Revolver was aimed at Roosevelt's chest. The bullet was slowed by a metal eyeglass case and a folded copy of his speech—those are what saved his life. For the rest of his life, the bullet would remain part of him, but he would finish his speech. Fortunate for him, his heart was protected.

Best Kicks

"Sneakerheads" is a term proudly proclaimed by a rising group of basketball shoe collectors. Some custom-made special kicks have gone for as much as $2 million. The MJ8's recently fetched $135K. I see guys at the gym show up with nice basketball shoes only to change to other basketball shoes when they play. The first ones were just for show. This is a growing sub-culture that is increasing in popularity on YouTube. They care what are on their feet.

Have your feet been fitted with the readiness of the gospel of peace? These are the most expensive shoes you will every wear. They are the best-fitting and the most effective. They are part of the full armor of God.

Ever go to a Trampoline Park? They make you buy "special" socks. I think the "special" part is how cheaply made they are for such a high price. They are not worth a nickel. You are allowed to keep them, but don't get too excited, they practically dissolve by the next day. But the footwear God has for you is very pricey. They are more than the Yeezys or the Kobes. Those can be bought with money, but these are only purchased with the blood of Jesus.

I remember my first pair of Jordans. I had had many pairs of "Jordaches," the knockoff brand. I went with my dad to a funeral, and I think it was in his heart to get me a new pair of ball shoes. After the service we went to the shoe store and he told me I could pick out any pair. I was a bit shy, but was eyeing those Jordans. I really wanted them, but the price was over $100. He saw my wanting them and grabbed them; we got them fitted and purchased. I felt so special. I did not play any better in them, but I knew they were valuable.

John the Baptist knew he was not even worthy to "tie Jesus' shoes." How much more valuable are the shoes purchased by His death?

At the bowling alley you've got to rent some footwear. Isn't the back of them always so hard? Blistering. But the shoes God gives us are the best-fitting. They are custom made.

The Brothers Grimm wrote stories that were much darker than the Disney movies. In Cinderella, the wicked step-sisters cut off part of their foot to try and make the glass slipper fit. The pool of blood gives them away. The gospel fits you. It is well worn. It has been broken in for the last 2000 years. They have "high ankle support," so you won't fall. Most of all, they are custom made for you. You know the same story of the "good news" of Jesus as any other Christian, but you have applied it to yourself. Your sins are forgiven. Your soul is empowered. No one looks like you.

"Buy our insoles product, it will make you jump five inches higher!" The promise of effectiveness is put at the forefront. The gospel gives us feet like "deer's feet." We have firm footing. Swiftly, we take the news of peace with us everywhere we go. In every country where there are Christians, there is a gospel witness. Missionaries, radio waves, and the precious name of Jesus has been exalted the world over and over.

Some hiking boots are "snakebite proof." You're safe from poisonous bites if you have their product. They are thick enough and strong enough to withstand the piercing teeth. But the gospel is not primarily defensive. "And the God of peace will soon crush Satan underneath your feet!" It's stomping time! We are called to trample on "snakes and scorpions." These shoes are awesome.

Years ago, I substituted for a very accomplished teacher. I knew he had multiple master's degrees, was working on a doctorate, and had many prestigious teachers' awards. I do not remember seeing any of them in his class, but one item was very important to him. There was a pair of old, worn out, white-turned-grey, wrinkled-like-a-raisin sneakers in a glass case. The inscription declared how those shoes had taken him to the USSR and all over the world preaching the gospel. That was his prized possession.

Shield of Faith

"Our arrows will blot out the sun," came the Persian threat.

"Then we will fight in the shade," was the bold reprise.

The Spartans had mastered the art of war and the use of shields. It was not only for the individual, but each soldier protected the one to their side.

"Take up the shield of faith, extinguishing the fiery arrows."

Your faith protects you. It protects those around you. It pushes the enemy back.

The Spartans had a mantra: "Come back with your shield—or on it." It was that important. Don't lose it. It will cause you disaster and disaster will spread to those around you. A soldier with a shield is clearly a soldier. As long as they bear it, no one would confuse their profession. A good solider does not get entangled in the affairs of this world, because they must strive to please the one who enlisted them.

Faith is what you believe. It is what you think about. Worldly concerns can't infiltrate. Darts fly, but don't break skin. They are wasted when the mind is occupied with the things of God.

Lot was fortunate he had his uncle Abraham praying for him. It was not Lot's righteousness or faith that saved him, but Abraham's.

Rahab's family was safe while their city of Jericho crashed to ashes. It was not due to them, but due to Rahab's faith.

Your faith, your prayers for those around you, greatly aids them. They may not even know how "lucky" they are. Shots are constantly being fired and your faith is knocking them out of the air. To hear "I have been praying for you" equals "how much worse things would have been" if not for them. The police and armed forces are always working around the clock. How bad would it be if they all disbanded?

My friend Jody got me this T-shirt of Jesus with a basketball doing a crossover and the devil falling over. The caption is "Not today, Satan." I love it. Faith pushes the enemy back. The shield wall advances. Captain America throws the shield. We push the evil one out of position.

The shield wall runs deep. If one falls, another is ready to take their place. If one is wounded, there is one standing by to help. The strength of each is multiplied by the whole. We run deep. If I can't preach a service, we have half a dozen preachers standing by at a moment's notice. Last Wednesday night my 17- year-old daughter was training two new worship team members with a combined age of 25. More shields being held. Our faith is contagious.

Helmet of Salvation

UFC 1 featured the introduction of Royce Gracie to the world. At 6'1" and 180 pounds, he was grossly outsized by Shootfighters, Sumo wrestlers, massive street fighters, and a field of huge contenders. His mastery of Brazilian Jiu-Jitsu was revolutionary to the fighting world. Although he would submit his opponents, his strikes would wear them down. More than punches or kicks, he threw the most effective head-butts. Forehead to face. Boom! Over and over at close quarters. Just imagine if he'd had a helmet on.

"Take up the helmet of salvation."

Gear up. Guard yourself. Go forward. When you've got your head covered, your thought-life will be sound.

Jim Rohn said it well: "Take care of your body. It's the only place you have to live." But there is another place we exist in our minds. When you are asleep, your body is limp, helpless, and disconnected, but your mind is still cognizant, in motion, moving, turning and making work. The man in the coma is still alive, he is still home, but not really in the body. He is more in the mind. Your perception is how you see the world. Protect it.

Football players have pre-game rituals. Smashing helmets, yelling and slapping the tops of each other's heads are their ways of readying up.

Think about your thought life. Remind yourself of salvation. You are saved. No, really, you are not under the wrath of God. How great is that? On your best day, that is the best news. On your worst day, that is the best news.

We are promised "the mind of Christ." If you are indwelt with His Spirit, you have access to His thoughts.

Eighty percent of all bike injuries could have been avoided if a helmet was worn. A good helmet absorbs the force of the enemy. In paintball, sometimes the best place to get shot is in the face...in the mask covering the face. It takes the brunt of it. Soldiers often find shrapnel that saved their life.

The little-leaguer has a new sense of confidence once that helmet comes on. It is not for cowards. It is not worn by the kids on the bench, but for the one facing the pitcher. There is a new cohesion. The whole unit wears the same helmet. The entire team supports the same colors.

Richard Bruno, a U.S. Marine, was ordered to protect a small Vietnam village in the heat of the war. With a handful of other soldiers, a few old men and a couple of teenagers, it looked like they had little hope of defending an attack. When the dreaded night came, Bruno exhausted his ammunition. In the heat of the chaos, his helmet fell off. Dread. An alert shook in his soul. He left cover, dove for it and in one motion, locked it on his head. No sooner was it covering him than a grenade exploded close by. In the morning, he would regain consciousness. They had won the battle. His helmet was full of shrapnel. It saved his life. He knew its importance.

The Sword of the Spirit

A gladiator is called such because the sword they swing is called a "gladius" in Latin. Their identity is intertwined with their weapon.

No matter their job, every U.S. Marine is first and foremost a rifleman. Their creed: "This is my rifle. There are many like it, but this one's mine. My rifle is my best friend. It is my life. I must master it as I must master my life. Without me, my rifle is useless; without it, I am useless..." They are serious about their weapon.

"And the Sword of the Spirit is the Word of God."

The sword must be taken. The sword must be learned. The sword must be swung.

Remember the story of Excalibur? Whoever is worthy, whoever is destined, will seize the sword and be king. Gideon had a son, Jether, who was too cowardly to even take up the weapon. He was mocked by defeated kings.

Swords are for warriors. They are for those who know there is a battle. And there is always a battle. We have a commission. Jesus came to "destroy the works of the devil." His strongholds seem to be growing. His power seems to be increasing. Jesus came, died, and rose, and now He has called us. We are the calvary. Will you take up yours? It is by hearing God's Word, reading it, and applying it to your life.

God's word is so powerful that it cuts the division of the spirit and the soul. Like any skill, it must be practiced. They say mastery is a ten-thousand-hour endeavor. How well do you know the Bible? If it is your primary weapon, what can be more important. It is a bit sad how many Christians can tell you the detailed stats about their favorite sports team, but are illiterate in the scriptures. Some will say "the Bible is difficult." Is it harder to understand than the rules of baseball or the strategy of football? We learn what we want to learn. Know your Bible. Develop your fighting style. How you quote it, how you converse about it, and how you proclaim it are all part of how you wield that weapon.

The sacred ground of Gettysburg was littered with guns, many of which had been loaded, not fired, then reloaded again and again. Men had been trained. They were armed. But they did not have it in them to pull the trigger. We hear God's word. We meditate on it. We are filled so that we can be emptied. We speak it. We pull that trigger. We are not "dumb dogs" that don't bark. We warn. We sound the alarm. There is power in God's word.

I was impressed the other day when I saw a clip of the TV show "America's Got Talent." There was a piano player who was hilariously talking about the different kinds of churches and how different ethnicities sing. He seemed to love God and have the light of life. I think I heard him say John 3:16 three times in two minutes. The audience enjoyed him, his voice, and style. But I loved that he delivered the word in such a powerful way.

Joshua: God Saves

General George Washington, General George Patton and General "Stormin' Norman" Schwarzkopf, are military leaders of renown. Some of America's best. But who is history's greatest General? Some may say Alexander the Great, or Napoleon or Genghis Khan. But I have one who I think is superior: Joshua, the servant of Moses. He was born a slave, but died in the promised land he conquered. Thirty-two kingdoms were toppled within 15 years.

Joshua experienced the power of God. He saw the plagues upon Pharaoh's land. He knew the promises that Abraham had received 400 years before. Faith over fear. But that faith had to endure 40 years of wandering in the wilderness while the doubters died. In that time, he learned from the best and became the servant of Moses. Victory after victory made him legendary.

After escaping Egypt, Moses entered the wilderness. He sent 12 spies into the land of Canaan, the land God had promised them. Ten of the spies came back with fearful reports. "We are like grasshoppers! They will devour us!" But Joshua and Caleb were of a different spirit. They believed the land was theirs and were excited to sleep in giant, king-size beds. But fear won the day. The congregation believed the ten spies, and God would punish them all for 40 years.

Joshua saw triumph before he had it. Napoleon was famous for his battle-ending predictions. He would say where and how a conflict would end with uncanny accuracy. His mind's eye was on replay when victory came. He had already seen it.

Moses left a few things undone. In the wilderness, he did not enforce circumcision, the sign of God's covenant. When Joshua crossed into enemy territory, he had all the men cut. Living right was more important than comfort or safety. It was at Gilgal, which means "roll away reproach" that Joshua renewed that covenant.

There were moments of doubt. Jericho was a huge, supernatural victory. God knocked the walls down after seven days and 13 laps of a silent walk-a-thon. But one of the soldiers, Achan, stole some of the accursed things. In the next battle, the army suffered their first and only loss. Joshua threw dust in the air and ripped his garment. He wanted to quit. "God, have you brought us this far to abandon us?" No. God needed the sin dealt with. God revealed the sin. Achan was stoned, and the army got back to its winning ways. Even great men of faith have doubts.

Before he led the army, Joshua served Moses. He was like his bodyguard. Where Moses went, Joshua went and waited. At the Tabernacle, Moses' face was glowing, and Joshua was waiting outside. When Moses received the Ten Commandments, Joshua was waiting at the bottom of the mountain.

Moses led. Joshua followed. When Moses died, the Lord buried him." But when Moses died, nothing of God died. Joshua became the leader. "As I was with Moses, so I will be with you," was the promise. The Kingdoms of Og, Sihon and Bashan fell to Moses...almost three dozen more would fall to Joshua. The Red Sea parted with Moses; the Jordan River parted with Joshua.

In the wilderness, with a rag-tag, poorly armed, unexperienced, fugitive slave force, Joshua led them to victories. They defeated walled cities, armored units, and veteran armies. In the promised land, Joshua unleashed excellent strategies and perfectly timed tactics. On two campaigns, he had initial slaughters that led to follow-up marches. Once the enemies' main forces were defeated, it was a rapid succession of attacking their cities. By the end of Joshua's life, he had removed the major strongholds from the promised land. He then divided it by tribe, and challenged them to conquer the rest.

The name "Joshua" means "Yah (the name of God) is salvation." He lived up to that name. He led his people into the promised land. Jesus, the son of God, was named after Joshua. Jesus is the greatest Savior ever!

Caleb: Exceptional

Archie Williams was a notable singer on America's Got Talent. He advanced. He got a standing ovation. The song he chose was especially powerful. There was a soul in his song seldom heard. It was not the notes he hit or the melody that rang out, but the heart behind it. For 37 years, Archie Williams had been incarcerated for a crime he never committed. In those unjust years, he maintained his innocence, prayed a lot and developed his singing voice. When he was exonerated by DNA evidence, his first stop was a nationally-televised singing competition. The crowd gave a roaring standing ovation as he sang "Don't Let the Sun Go Down on Me" by Elton John. His attitude after unjustly losing his freedom for 37 years was exceptional, and he sang the song with the force of conviction that only long years can make.

The book of Numbers is a funny book. Out of all the stats cataloged, all the thousands of men from each tribe, the important number is two. Because only two men survived the Exodus. Joshua was one. Caleb was the other. He was the other spy that had a good report.

Caleb held a promise for a long time. He held his legacy for a long time. He held onto "another spirit" for a long time.

"Do not grow weary of doing well, you will reap a reward in due time," the Apostle Paul writes the Galatians. For 40 years, Joshua carried hope. They travelled in circles, almost aimlessly, waiting, dying. Tents, clothes, weapons, might have been heavy, but hope was light. It gave him energy.

Caleb could have gotten bitter. He believed. It was the doubt of the ten spies that made him suffer. Unjust. But hope can dissipate that darkness. He knew there was better. It is one thing to never ride first class and enjoy coach, but when you have gone first class one time, it is hard not to envy those big seats. It is almost better not to have the best, because if you can't keep having it, you will enjoy everything else less. Not Caleb. He saw the best of the land, and every day delighted in daydreaming about his return. Hope…hope.

Caleb knew war. He was strong for battle. In the wilderness, he had helped topple several kingdoms. There was a hill that he claimed. A walled city sat on its beacon: Kirjath Sepher. That would be his home and the home of his children for generations to come. He was more than 80 years old when his chance came, but he had the strength of his youth. He conquered much, but he left it as a challenge to his future son-in-law. "Whoever takes that city can marry my daughter." This ensured his legacy would be warriors. Othniel the son of

Kenaz, became that hero. When Chushan-rishathaim, the King of Mesopotamia invaded, he took up the sword to save the nation. In his wilderness time, he planned for generations to come.

Everyone begins uniquely. The creativity in children is awesome. "Kids Say the Darndest Things" could be a TV show. But then they conform. We educate the creativity out of them. But Caleb was of "another spirit." He never lost that. The doubt of the masses could not take it. The bitterness of years wasted could not take it. His hope was too powerful. His spirit could not be tainted.

There is a bronze statue of a Canadian with a Bible in one hand and a dental tool in the other, standing by the Tamsui River in New Taipei City. The nation recently celebrated the 150th anniversary of the missionary George Leslie Mackay. There is a "Mackay Street," a hospital, a museum, and even a college with his plaques. Mackay arrived in Taiwan on December 29th, 1871. Unlike many missionaries at the time, he took to the customs and culture of his new country. Quickly he learned the language and ate the food. He even married a local woman and raised his kids there. For decades, he planted churches, taught the best methods of medical and dental procedures, and served the people. He was famous for the joy he brought to the hospitals he founded. His church choirs would fill the suffering halls with life. He so impacted Taiwan, that even a century-and-a-half later he is honored there.

Othniel: Be Seized

With his white ninja suit and two katana blades, Storm Shadow was my favorite G.I. Joe. I would get lost in a world of my imagination, setting up Duke, Bazooka and Cobra Commander. The odds were 50-1, Storm Shadow was surrounded. Dozens of guns were pointed right at him. A tank, a machine-gun-toting jeep and a chopper were all ready to attack him. He seemingly had no chance. However, I was controlling all the action. He was in my hand. Within moments, Storm Shadow would be the only one standing. Even the vehicles had been flipped. Victory depended on who was in my hand. So it is with God, if only we can be held by Him.

The name "Othniel" means "seized by God." When an invader came into Israel, he was the first judge to lead the charge. He won victories, threw off the oppressors, married Caleb's daughter and brought peace to the nation.

He knew what was promised. He knew the Holy Spirit. He knew the presence of God.

Before David fought Goliath, he asked what a champion would receive. Before Othniel took the city Kirjath Sepher, he listened to what the offer was. After his conquest, he got to inherit the land and come into Caleb's family. He asked for even more land. Kirjath Sepher had a massive library in it. After the conquest, Othniel renamed it "Debir" which means "Sanctuary." That is how we learn God's promises. Take God's book and make it your sanctuary. Know what God has promised you.

Because he married into Caleb's family, Othniel got to spend time with him. Champions grow around other champions. Courage is contagious. Learning is contagious. Doers spend time with doers.

God's Spirit came upon him. This is the source of his power. "Where the Spirit of the Lord is, there is freedom." "God has not given us a spirit of fear, but of power, love and a sound mind." It is when the Holy Spirit comes upon you that you are empowered to be a witness. That Spirit is still available for us. Do you know the power of the Holy Spirit? We are to be "led" by the Spirit and know the mind of the Spirit. He guides us. He is the Advocate that Jesus promised. We are so thankful and excited to be baptized with Him because we see glimpses of Him in the lives of mighty men like Othniel.

There are many opponents to God and His Kingdom. God is using people to fulfill His purposes and His promises. If you are willing to serve the Lord, you will know His presence.

Ted Williams was the greatest hitter in MLB history. He is a Hall-of-Famer and a Red Sox legend. In the prime of his career, he would miss five years. As much as he loved his baseball uniform, in his heart he was a marine. He served in WWII and in Korea, flying 39 missions. He was the wingman for future astronaut, John Glenn. The bonds of playing catch paled to his military obligations. The victories in the diamond were small compared to the victories on the battlefield. God has a greater calling for you. His promises are greater, His Spirit is greater and His presence is greater.

Ehud: Unsuspecting Swords

Road rage is a bad idea where I live in So-Ca. You never know who is armed.

Picking random fights is also a terrible idea. There are more and more MMA fans and unsuspecting practitioners. You really never know who is secretly dangerous.

Ehud only had one arm. Maybe it was his unassuming demeanor that made him a candidate for the tribute-bringing. Annually, he brought the loot Israel paid invading King Eglon of Moab. God gave him a mission—a mission to assassinate and overthrow the oppressor. A custom dagger was fashioned. It was a cubit long, and fit under his right thigh. The next time tribute was paid, Eglon would get a tip.

The cold sweat and nerves overwhelmed Ehud. He came to the palace intent on ending the heathen king, but never found an opportunity. Before he could do the deed, he was out the door with a "thank you very much." Regret. Self-disappointment. Self-disgust. How could he have been so cowardly? His people depended on him. His feet took him to the city of Gilgal. The moonlight illuminated a large pile of rocks in the center of the city. The smooth stones were once under the Jordan River, but reminded him of how God had used Joshua to enter the promised land. They had not lost that promise. He only needed to be reminded, and with that, he turned around and headed back. His pace hastened.

A banging at the palace door. "Oh, it is Ehud...come in. The King is up on the roof. I am sure he would love to see you after that great gift you brought earlier." The Moabite King welcomed his long-subdued servant as they overlooked the city. "I have a message for you. It is a message from our God. I need to tell you. I need to tell you in private." The guards were dismissed. A one-armed man was hardly a threat. They had long stopped searching him for weapons. How wrong they were! Once alone, Ehud leaned in to whisper as if only Eglon was worthy of this great mystery. Leaning in, Eglon, anticipating and smirking at what he thought would be certain good news, a sharp pain burst from his stomach. "Something I ate?" he thought. An instant later, the pain was unbearable. He looked. Shock. A red waterfall splashing onto a reflecting pond of blood. The message had come. It was sharp. And it would be his end. The dagger would not come out, so Ehud left it in. His knowledge of the palace now came into play. He escaped to rally his people. The trumpet blew before Eglon's men knew he was dead. A revolution began with Israel regaining their freedom because of a one-armed man.

God uses our weaknesses. God uses our courage. We are to use God's word.

"My power is perfected in weakness," the Apostle Paul writes. It is ironic that a left-handed man is from the tribe of Benjamin, because the name Benjamin means "son of my right hand." No one else could have gotten that blade through the palace bodyguards. God had the right person in the right place.

Sometimes we have to be reminded of past victories to gain courage. At Gilgal he turned back. The name "Gilgal" means to roll away. It was not only the place Joshua had the rocks stacked, but was the place he had the nation circumcised. There was reproach for their disobedience of not keeping the covenant God had given to Abraham. It was there that it was rolled away. Courage can come back. Shame can be cast out. After blowing the trumpet, Ehud yelled "Follow me!" What a liberating cry! It was not "We need more tribute for Eglon." It was "Eglon is dead! Let's throw off this oppression! Follow me!" What a different shout!

The Word of God is a double-edged blade. It cuts to the spirit and soul. Eglon was a fat man. He was a ginormous bumba. The blade could not be pulled out. His rolls fell upon it. His insides were falling out. And it was ugly. If our inner sins were put on the outside, how hideous that would be.

It is unexpected when the youngest sibling orders the others around. You would not expect teenagers to be beholden to a kindergartner. But it happens when the parents have given a message through that kid to the older ones. They say it proudly and boldly. "...Mom and Dad said." That is the game-changer. You, too, will have confidence and courage when you use God's word. Even our weaknesses can be overcome.

Shamgar: Resourceful

In the days of King Solomon, gold was as common as brass. Gold shields were carved and placed in the temple. In the apostasy following Solomon, the temple was raided by Sheshank, the King of Egypt. Those shields were taken. The next king would replace them with bronze ones. Hundreds of years later, Jehoiada the priest would overthrow the wicked Queen Athaliah. As he anointed a new king in the temple, she tried to interrupt, but he had armed guards with those bronze shields that slew her. He used what was available.

Shamgar came after Ehud. In the days of Philistine oppression no one went outside. No one walked the streets. No one but

Shamgar. He did not have a proper weapon, but used what he had, an oxgoad. This eight-to-twelve-foot-long stick had a spike on one side and a spade, like a shovel on the other. Its primary use was herding cattle. You could prick the animal from a safe distance. But for Shamgar, the primary purpose was pulverizing Philistines. Six hundred fell at his unorthodox style.

Keep walking. Keep succeeding. Keep serving.

Shamgar did not walk like everyone else. While they cowered in their homes, he marched boldly down deserted highways. We walk by faith, not by sight. Situations are not what stop us. Adversaries are not what stop us. We tread. We overcome with what we have. The Spirit of God leads us. We don't walk like we did before we were indwelt. It is not our ego driving us, but a humility that loves justice and kindness.

A friend of mine was a drug and alcohol counselor. When people got DUIs they would find themselves mandated to his office. Many, many times he would share his faith. On occasion, someone would get hostile and offended. He would listen to them and their opinions and hate of God, and then gently ask the piercing question, "How is that working for you? Obviously, if you are seeing me, in trouble with the law, not too well." They were stubborn to hold onto foolish ways. We are stubborn in succeeding. We go from glory to glory.

Every Olympic Gold Medalist has a treasure trove of lesser awards. This is not their first rodeo. They were prodigies as children, high school superstars, college standouts, and likely at the top one percent of their professional sport. We are like that, more than overcomers. God uses us in unusual ways.

The retired firefighter cannot remember all the people he saved. The paramedic revives and rescues person after person. The preacher sees salvation after salvation, baptism after baptism. It is about saving.

Shamgar's people were scared, but he wasn't. He refused to be. His people were lost, but he wasn't. He refused to be. His people were savable, they needed him to be him.

Thomas Hawkes suffered a dramatic martyrdom. He was born into a good family in England and attended higher education, but refused to have his son baptized into the Catholic church. It was during a time of Protestant persecution. He was sentenced to be burned at the stake. The night before his execution, he was visited by some fellow Christian friends. They were worried if they had to die for their faith that it would be too much. "Give us a signal if it is too much...too painful, put your hands up." When the pile was lit, Thomas' face remained unfazed. As the fire burned brighter, his hands began to slowly move up. His friends' hearts stopped. "Oh no, it is too much," they thought. But then his countenance changed. A smile came over him. His hands began to clap. The last burst of energy showed his friends that there is a glory in suffering. That if they had to, there would be a special grace for them too.

Barak: Get up

Big Days Day School requires an early alarm. Not only does it ring next to the youth, but both mom and dad have their phones set. The sin of snooze is hit. Fortunately, dad awakens and knocks on the door. Though startled, the youth quickly goes back to sleep. Minutes later mom is readying breakfast wondering where they are. "Get up, get up!" echoes down the hall. Finally, a frustrated dad shakes the student. "Get up or you will be late!" God has been doing this to some of us. He has called us to rise up. He has sent people to stir us. It is time we get up.

After years of Canaanite oppression, it was past time for a hero to emerge. But what does God do when the one He is calling does not get up? He calls others. Deborah, the prophetess, the judge, the woman of God, knew that God had long been calling Barak to lead the troops. God had used lesser-known men like Ehud and Shamgar, and now it was getting annoying. "Barak, Barak, get up. Hasn't God been calling you?" He was fearful. "I will go lead the army, but only if you come with me." "I will, but your conditions have a cost. A woman will get the glory from the victory God will give you."

The trumpet was blown. Ten thousand men answered his call. The best warriors from Naphtali and Zebulun came ready to win. In opposition, Jabin the King of Canaan, sent his general Sisera with 900 iron chariots to meet the rag-tag military. God would intervene. As the chariots rumbled the ground, the clouds changed. The sky switched to gray. It was not the storm season. Travelling by wadi was as good as a freeway, until the rains started pouring. Thunder shook the hearts of the charioteers. Hail began falling. Wheels were spinning off axels. Others were getting stuck in the mud. The Canaanite soldiers lifted their shields to stop the crazy weather. Barak charged down the mountain. Victory would be his.

You are already called. You can lose your blessing, but you can still win.

Do you find putting the last puzzle piece in the puzzle satisfying? Isn't it perfect when you are doing exactly what you know you were made to do? God has never changed His mind. "The gifts and callings of God are without repentance." What God has called you to, He has still called you to. Have you listened to God? Are you doing what you ought to be doing? Other people will confirm it. You will be fulfilled doing it. Once you know why you are on this planet, the rest of life is simply doing it. Barak was late, but not too late.

Esau was blessed until he forfeited his blessing. He traded his birthright for a bowl of stew. Twelve spies entered the promised land and only two would be blessed for their optimistic faith. Ten would be cursed for their doubt at God's promise. Disobedience will cost you blessings.

A dad wanted to take his son to the movies after work. But arriving home, he found the boy was in trouble for not doing his chores, not doing his homework and teasing his sister. Rather than a movie, the kid got a spanking and a grounding. He lost a blessing he did not even know he could have had. Sometimes we wonder how much better life could have been had we walked in obedience to God sooner.

"Out!"—the umpire pumped his thumb up over his shoulder. Although he led the league in stolen bases and was the fastest runner, this time he was caught. The problem? He got the steal signal late. Late can cost you. It cost Barak.

Do you ever feel like life has passed you by? That can be a sad thought. That can lead to mid-life crises. It hasn't passed you by. It isn't too late to follow God. It is not too late to grow in Christ. Barak did advance. He is a hero of the faith. God had gone before him. Hebrews records him as a hero of the faith.

Many great quarterbacks came later in life to the NFL. Kurt Warner was 28 when he entered the league. After college he was bagging groceries before playing in the arena league. That led to a year in the European League and finally, to the big show. His incredible journey would see him win a Super Bowl and earn two MVP awards. With his superstar status he did more charity work and was recognized with the Walter Payton NFL Man of the Year Award. His faith in Jesus has always been at the forefront. Fans and Christians look back on his football career as a great success, even if it took years to get there.

Deborah: Lead Well

My wife wears many hats. She is a powerful woman of God. She is a wife, a mother to four unique, beloved kids, a pastor, a speaker, a designer, a sister and a thoughtful friend, to name a few. Great women often are many things. Deborah was one such woman. "Now Deborah, a prophetess and the wife of Lapidoth, was judging Israel at that time." We've just met her and we are impressed with her resumé.

Deborah shows us how to lead where you are, go where you are needed and encourage others where to go.

Our church runs basketball leagues. It is a good hook to bring people to Christ. We hire the best ref, have a scoreboard, free food, music, an announcer and jerseys. Although it is outside on a short full court, it is always a great competition. More than the games, are the teams. Each week we have a written devotional that teams read together. Then they pray one for another. It is awesome! As I prayerfully make the teams, I consider who is a good leader, a good player and a good teammate. They have to be several things. "Let the one who leads, lead with zeal and excellence," the Apostle Paul wrote to the Romans.

Deborah lived between Ramah and Bethel. Ramah represented the heathen "high places" of worship. "Bethel" means "the house of God." This is where we often find ourselves: between this world and God. We are in this world but not of this world. Anywhere we go, we can hear God. He is closer than our cell phones. Deborah would travel teaching God's word and administering justice. She was calling the people "up."

Barak's requirement, "I will go if you go with me," was met with "then we go together." She was ready and willing to go. Her next line would be a difficult one to say. "Because you would not go alone, God will take the glory of victory from you and give it to a woman." We go where we are needed and we say what needs to be said. Because of her boldness and responsiveness, she was called "a mother of Israel."

John Maxwell said it well: "Leaders know what is next." Deborah knew what God wanted to do, where He wanted to do it and who He wanted to use. She would praise God for the victory.

Deborah wrote a beautiful song about the battle and its outcome. It could be entitled: "My heart is with those who willingly offer themselves." Some fought with all their might. Some came from far away and brought their best effort.

Equally, she remembers those who did not attend. The city of Meroz is cursed for their absence. Some caused "searching of hearts" for being too busy or being too scared. Out of all things you are, I want to encourage to you to always be present.

Jael: Easy Opportunities

A man lived by a plaza. In haste to get home, he stopped in the liquor store to grab some orange juice that his wife had requested. "How much was this?" she asked seeing the small paper bag. "Umm, umm $5.50." "That is too much. Take it back...they are on sale at the super market for $2.50. Go get one from there." Without taking off his shoes, he dashed out the door and returned to the liquor store. As he returned the juice, he noticed a lit up sign announcing that the lottery was over $315 million. Instead of keeping the change, he bought two lotto tickets. He liked Jack in the Bean Stalk too much. That night as his wife was scolding him, the lucky numbers were read and he won! It was too easy.

Everything that could have gone wrong for Sisera, did. His chariots were stuck, his men were running and hail was attacking. Looking for shelter, he ran to the tents of the Kenites who were neutral in the conflict. They were the descendants of Abraham through his late wife, Keturah. Heber was the chief, but he was not home at the time of Sisera's desperate flight. His wife Jael, was. "Hide me. Hide me. I have been defeated. Please don't let anyone know I am here." "Ok. Let me get you something to drink." "Water. Water. I am so, so thirsty." Rather, she brought him some warm milk. With a heavy stomach and exhausted legs, he quickly fell asleep. She covered his head with a blanket. Then she crept to the workman's hammer. It was a mallet used to beat the long tent pegs into the ground to secure the heavy tents. She grabbed a tent peg. Slowly. Quietly. She came to where his head was laid. She aligned the spike with Sisera's temple....and "POW!!!" One strike and his head was tented. Just then, Deborah and Barak were coming by looking for their defeated enemy. Jael got the glory. She killed the enemy general. Opportunity was that easy.

Opportunities are arriving. Honor is awaiting. Obedience is expected.

Be open to what God is doing. There are many subplots to His grand story. Jael was not a main character until the opportunity came. She was ready because she was resourceful. Remember Ehud made a dagger. Remember Shamgar used a farm tool. She joins their ranks as a creative hero. She was also decisive. It is likely her family was neutral in the conflict. Some have recorded that her husband had been hired to build some of the war chariots. But she smashed his business deal. There was no turning back.

"Seek honor. Seek immortality. Seek God persistently," the Apostle Paul writes. Others are watching. They will be inspired to live honorably. Barak forfeited the honor because he hesitated. Jael received it because she acted immediately. You may not have a sword, but you have a weapon.

"Blessed is Jael above all women in the tent," Deborah praised. She saw an opportunity and she nailed it!

I heard a terrible story of a waitress that was tipped a lottery ticket. It won her ten million dollars. She was swiftly fired for not sharing. Then she was sued by her fellow waitresses and cooks, and an ex-boyfriend kidnapped her. When she was rescued, the IRS came after her. Winning was the worst thing that happened to her. There is an opportunity the world offers that ends in suffering and death. There is an opportunity God offers that adds wealth with no sorrow.

Gideon: Does Motive Matter?

In 1969, Clara Hale became "Mother Hale." With a heart for those who needed a home, she opened hers. Within a few years she was serving several homes and running a major operation. Unfortunately, her greedy daughter would take over and embezzle almost half a million dollars. It started well, but would end in disgrace. Gideon was a story like that.

Seven long years of being oppressed would lead to Gideon becoming a hero. Each harvest, the Midianites would come up like locust and devour everything. The cry of suffering was loud in the ears of God. "Mighty man, you will lead your people to victory!"—God spoke to Gideon. "Who me? Couldn't be." He was from the smallest tribe, smallest clan, and smallest family, but God would use him. To assure him, God allowed him two tests. There was dew on the ground, but not a fleece and then the opposite. Convinced God was with him, he blew the trumpet and 32,000 warriors answered the call. "Too many," God began, "They will get the glory." So Gideon offered any cowards to go home, and instantly 22,000 hit the bricks. "Still too many." Gideon took them to the brook to drink. Only 300 stayed alert and drank from cupped hands. "That is your army." Gideon was given one more assurance. He overheard some Midianite guards interpreting a dream that had a "barley loaf" crushing their tents.

God gave Gideon a plan, but not a chant. With torches in jars, the flame was concealed. The 300 surrounded the Midianite camp of 135,000. At Gideon's signal, they all shattered their jars, shone their light and yelled "The sword of the Lord and of Gideon!" Be mindful, Gideon did not even have a sword at this point. They charged in. Confusion filled the camp. Chaos broke out. Man turned on man. It was a self-inflicted bloodbath. Gideon blew another trumpet and rallied more soldiers. Midianite kings would fall. Gideon had revenge on his mind. With passion, he pursued Zebah and Zalmunna for miles. Two different cities refused to help him. "I'll remember this," Gideon threatened. With a surprise attack, Gideon defeated the last 15,000 and took those two kings captive. He would run them through and punish the cities of Succoth and Peniel.

When the smoke settled, Gideon was a great hero. "Be our king," the masses demanded. "Not me. Not my sons. The Lord is your King," he replied. It sounded right, but his heart was not right. He asked for their facial gold (earrings, nose rings and the like). It was a fortune. With it, he made an idol. It was a golden vest. The nation came to worship it. He also hired lots of prostitutes. He would have 70 sons, one of whom was Abimelech, whose name means "my father is king." National apostasy would set in and Gideon's sons would have a bloody end. The end was worse than the beginning.

Don't doubt. Don't boast. Don't make God's victory about vengeance.

Faith is contagious; so is fear. You choose. If you have faith of a mustard seed, you can move a mountain. Gideon is called, but he has some questions for God: "Why has all this happened and where are all the miracles my father's told me about?" God had to keep reassuring him. Before he would deliver his people, he would chop down the statues of Baal and Ashura at his father's house. He waited until night and did it in secret.

Boasting leads to arrogance. It shows a braggadocious heart. There were too many. If 32,000 would have won, they would have said "We are great soldiers." If 10,000 would have won, they would have praised themselves, "We are great tacticians." But with only 300, all had to worship "We have a great God!" Their provisions were thin…pathetic. A few jars and torches. But then to yell "The sword of the Lord and Gideon!"—as if Gideon was equal to the Lord.

God wanted a liberating victory; Gideon got greedy. He was bitter. Years before, Zebah and Zalmunna had killed his brothers. This pursuit was something he had long dreamed of. He got everything he wanted, but in the end it was destructive.

In Orpah of the Abiezrites, there was a home with three monuments. A pile of rubble contained what was the face of Baal and the hand of Ashura. A cobweb pile of rocks was once the altar to "Jehovah Shalom." And then, there was a glittering, dazzling golden vest where all the nation came to worship. The end was worse than the beginning.

Abimelech: When the Wrong Men Suit Up

On July 23, 2011 a deranged 32-year-old Norwegian posed as a police officer on Utøya Island. By the day's end, he would open fire and kill more than 70 people. His animosity and slaying of the innocent sent shockwaves throughout Europe. It is reminiscent of Abimelech the son of Gideon, who would slay 68 of his brothers on one stone.

After Gideon died, the nation mourned their hero. Abimelech was his son, but his mother was a stranger, perhaps a prostitute. He stayed with her. Seeing the void of leadership, he convinced his mother's family to support him as ruler. "Better me, someone you know, someone who is like you, better just me than to have all of Gideon's sons ruling." They were convinced. Money from the temple of Baal-Berith was secured. Abimelech hired a band of scoundrels. They attacked Gideon's home at Orpah. One half-brother escaped, but the rest were killed upon one stone. From a hill a safe distance away, Jotham, Gideon's other son, shouted a story. "The trees of the forest looked for a king. They went to the olive tree, but he was too busy pleasing God and being useful to people. Likewise, the vines and the fig tree. However, the Bramble Bush—the thorns, volunteered. "May fire come from you and consume your followers and may fire from your followers consume you." For the next three years he terrorized his own people.

When men were gossiping about him in Shechem, he attacked his own city and razed it to the ground. And then with malice, he sowed it with salt. Thebez looked like it was going to rebel. Likewise, he attacked. Citizens ran to the tower for refuge. At Shechem, he had burned the tower full of people. "Get briars, bramble and burnable things. Set them at the base of the tower." As he went to light it up, a certain woman dropped a millstone on his head. The blow was thought to be fatal. Panic. Fear. Dread. Embarrassment. He looked in terror to his servant. "Run me through. End my life. I do not want people to say "He was killed by a woman." But what do we remember about Abimelech? He was killed by a woman.

A porcupine spike is not bad compared to a cobra bite. By comparison, we can make anything good or anything bad. Abimelech is a manipulator. "Choose me because I am better." It is "better" to have one ruler than many. It is "better" to have a ruler that looks like you and is from where you are from. He plays to ugly tribalism.

I knew a man that was a coach, and he was a bad coach. Why was he bad? He was a poor decision-maker. In games, he did not play the right players. If any of his stars made a mistake, he would instantly pull them out and yell at them. He had varsity talent on a freshmen team. He lost one of the games on purpose because he wanted to show a few parents how bad their kids were, so he sat out his best ones. It was painful to watch him all season. Practices were a near waste of time and his treatment of the kids was discouraging. Abimelech was like that. This guy was a lousy leader. He kills his brothers, attacks his own city and is limited on ideas. Why do kids bite when they get into a fight? It is because that is what worked when they were babies. They have not grown sense.

"When the wicked rule, the people mourn," the proverb goes. Where were the right guys? Why didn't they stand up? It does not take much for wicked men to deceive when no one stands against them. Sheep without a sheepdog are at the mercy of the wolves.

Doug Livent was an off-duty officer who heard some commotion. A three-year-old had fallen into a pool unattended. By the time he arrived, the boy was motionless. In moments, he dove in and pulled the boy out. CPR was performed. Moments were like hours. Then, suddenly, the prayers were answered and the boy was revived. "Thank you, thank you, thank you. You saved our son!" He was happy to help. When the media heard and interviewed him, he said "It's a God thing. God put strong people in the right place." We are fortunate to be strong enough to help others.

Tola: Worms That Save

Franklin D. Roosevelt was the 32nd President of the United States. He presided from 1933-1945, longer than any other president. He governed through the Great Depression up into World War II. His vast achievements were all done with paralyzed legs. He made the New Deal from a wheel chair. He was an unexpected leader that brought America to new levels of prosperity. Tola was like that.

After Abimelech, the nation was in a mess. But God would send them an unexpected savior. "Then after him was Tola, a man of Issachar, the son of Puah, the son of Dodo, he arose to save Israel. He lived in Shamir, in the hill country of Ephraim. He led the nation for 23 years, then he died and was buried in Shamir." That is it. He arose to save. His name means "worm." A worm saved.

Fill the void. Be faithful at home. Fulfill your calling.

We were made to clean up. A baby makes a mess. Moms and dads clean up after them. Kids break things. Moms and dads fix things. Teenagers re-arrange things. Moms and dads re-re-arrange them. We can help. If you are reading this, you have the ability to be part of the solution.

A 99-year-old Italian man recently divorced his 97-year-old wife. While cleaning out some papers in the attic, he had found some love letters written by a man she had an affair with some 60 years earlier. He could not stand her unfaithfulness for a day. Tola was faithful at home. He led from his family to his clan, to his tribe to his nation. Be steady for a long time. When it is difficult, stay faithful. The name "Shamir" means the place of thorns. Not easy. But saving the nation shouldn't be.

Tola saved. He arose with courage and consistency. He reminds us of Psalm 22, a Messianic prophecy, pointing to Christ. "I am a worm, not a man." There came another one who saved. Jesus. Beaten. Hung on a cross, mocked, and ridiculed, He felt like a worm, not a man. But He arose, and now He, too, saves.

Jair: Decorative

The worst player on my high school baseball team was always the dirtiest. He was embarrassed that he rarely got into the game. His parents were not able to watch. After the games, his spotlessly clean jersey would get grass stained as he would randomly dive and slide to make it look like he had worked hard. He could have gone the entire season without washing it and it would not have smelled. But he wanted the appearance of a hard worker without doing the work.

After Tola, there was Jair. He had 30 sons who rode on 30 donkeys who reigned over 30 towns. It sounds impressive. It must have been a scene when they rode into town. A generation later, the nation would need a general and, unfortunately, none of Jair's silver-spoon-fed sons would be qualified. Unused armor depreciates. Unused armor diminishes. Unused armor can destroy.

The old adage is true: "Use it or lose it." Jesus taught it like this: "To those that have, more is given. To those that don't have, even what little they do have is taken away." There is armor that is custom made for you. If you don't use it, it will not fit someone else. You don't wear someone else's blackbelt or letterman's jacket. Even if you see a nice one at a thrift store, you are unlikely to purchase one. If you never fight a battle, why do you have armor? If you have a ball bag with a custom bat, glove and batting glove, but you never play, it's worth less than you bought it for.

Thirty cities sounds like a lot, but if you knew that Jair's family used to be in charge of sixty cities, perhaps you would be disappointed. The balloon is still high, but it is losing air and it used to be higher. There are many comfortable losers out there. They have less than their fathers, but enough for themselves. They know their children will have less than them, and it does not bother them.

My old college basketball jersey doesn't fit me anymore. It was good for 185 pounds, but my new heavyweight 240-pound frame, not so much. If you change and your armor doesn't, it isn't going to fit.

Faith in the unfaithful is like a broken tooth or a dislocated ankle. If you don't know how to use a handgun, don't own one. An experienced crook will take it away and use it properly against you. If you have a firearm, get trained with it. King David refused Saul's armor. It would not fit him and he did not trust it. He won against Goliath in part because he would not take on someone's armor.

50

A typewriter sold for $254,000. It was not new. It was used. Used by Cormac McCarthy, the author of "All the Pretty Horses," "No Country for Old Men," and "The Road," to name a few. He used that typewriter and it became more valuable. What is worth more money: A pair of Jordan Brand shoes or a pair of Michael Jordan's shoes that he wore in the NBA Championship? Use what you have and it will multiply and grow in value.

Jephthah: Might and Weakness

Everyone loves a Cinderella story. Perhaps the best one in the Bible is Jephthah. "Jephthah was a mighty man of valor, but his mother was a prostitute." Teased. Taunted. They were so cruel. His brothers ran him out of town so he would not get any of the inheritance. He escaped 80 miles away to the land of Tob. There, he rustled up a gang of "worthless" cutthroats. They raided. They pillaged. They fought, tussled and showed their toughness. Back home, his brothers faced the threat of an Ammonite invasion. Without a leader or warrior among them, they desperately reached out to Jephthah. Humbly, they made the journey and pleaded with him to help.

Jephthah was willing, but he wanted to seek God. He went with them, but they stopped in Mizpah, where the ark of the covenant was. He poured out his heart. Forgiveness. Reconciliation. Hope.

When the family reunited at home, they met Jephthah's daughter and he got to work. Jephthah was well-versed in Israel's history, as well as Ammonite history. He wrote an articulate letter declaring that the Ammonites had no claim to the land of the Israelites. He wrote that they could have what their god Chemosh gives them, and if they continued, they would be fighting the God of Israel, the Great Judge. The letter was scorned, crumpled and ignored. But the Holy Spirit came upon Jephthah. Victory after victory. Twenty-two battles in a row. Perhaps it was his old insecurities, but Jephthah could not believe his success. He bartered with God. "If you will give me total victory, I will give you the first living thing that comes from my home as a burnt offering." In those days, many lived on the second floor and kept animals on the first. It was a foolish vow. Victory would be total. As his parade came through his hometown, his heart all but stopped. He watched his house, thinking a cow or a goat or a sheep would be the first animal to exit, but it wasn't. "NOOOO! Daughter, why have you brought me so low?" She was his one and only child. He explained his vow, she only asked for a few months to be with her friends. That was granted and then his vow was carried out.

In his mourning, the tribe of Ephraim gave Jephthah added grief. "Why didn't you invite us to the battle? You know we love to fight." Jephthah was in no mood. A civil war broke out. With all his love of history, it's too bad he did not take a note from Gideon on how to deal with the Ephraimites. Jephthah won the battle and took over the river crossings. When the Ephraimites got caught, Jephthah would check their accent. If they failed, he executed them. Forty-two thousand Ephraimites died that day.

Jephthah understood about might and about weakness. His pen was mighty, the Holy Spirit was mighty, but his decisions were weak.

The name Jephthah means "be open." Be open to God using you. Be open to what you write, what you pray and what you do, making a great impact.

"The pen is mightier than the sword." By the pen, armies march. One stroke of ink signs a death warrant, agrees to a hit, and declares a war. Know how to write. Know your history. Know your opponent's history. Every coach knows their players' strong points, and they get film on their adversaries' weaknesses.

It was God who gave Jephthah victory. We too are overcomers. As a dad, I used to let my kids win in the video games. Sometimes they were so bad, I had to try hard to lose. Now, I think they let me win. God causes us to triumph. His presence keeps us going. Jephthah stayed anointed. He stayed empowered.

You can have great knowledge and the power of the Holy Spirit and still make bad decisions. That sounds so wrong, but it is true. It is a terrible idea to barter for something that is free. If a king gives you a gift you could never afford, it would be insulting to offer them a "trade" for the piece of folded gum in your pocket. Receive it. Don't argue with angry people. It cost 42,000 lives.

A few nights ago, we were coming home from Idyllwild. Our car was empowered. The stars shined brightly in the night. As we winded down the mountain I did not see a car behind us or oncoming for a while. Then, out of nowhere, there was a mobile traffic light. I felt like someone was playing a joke on me. It was late. There was no roadwork going on. No sirens. Nothing. I know the laws of the road. I have knowledge. I have gas in the vehicle, I had power. I waited. My kids were asleep. A few moments went by. I was sitting in my mini-van, waiting. A minute went by, another, another, and then another... nothing. I was tempted to just drive. I was not sure it was going to change. Maybe it got left on red. Maybe it was a mistake, a joke? I almost went. Then I saw head lights coming at us. Three cars passed. The light turned green. We drove around a bend for about a mile, then we came to where both lanes became one. A few moments later there was another light with cars waiting to go. I was glad we waited. It would have been a disaster had I gone. Jephthah had power and knowledge, but made bad choices that caused a disaster.

Ibzan, Elon, Abdon: Forgettable

"The mass of men lead lives of quiet desperation," wrote Henry David Thoreau. Let that sink in..."quiet desperation."

After Jephthah's battles and six short years of judging, the nation would be led by three forgettable men. Ibzan, Elon and Abdon were quiet, brief and forgettable.

Ibzan had 30 sons and 30 daughters and he traded them. Elon led for ten years. Elon lived and died in Aijalon. No battles. No enemies. No glory. No challenges, no champions. All comfort, no change. No courage, no continuing.

Leaders, you are called to lead through and lead to. Tough times require tough leaders. Each of us is called to a cause. There is something bigger than ourselves. Ibzan had a big family. But we've got to get beyond our family. Start there and keep going.

Some people believe their best days are behind them. I will never believe that. Forward. Next. Better. Improve.

Eating potato chips and drinking sodas on the couch is not going to improve you. There is no revival. There is no expansion. Armor was never taken out, dented or used.

What kind of legacy do you want to leave? Where do you want to show your courage?

Willam James Sidis was born in 1898. He was a genius. By 18 months old, he was reading the New York Times. Within a few years he was speaking eight languages. Ivy league schools were recruiting him. At 11, he was attending Harvard, studying mathematics and giving lectures. The world awaited what he would become. But he did not like the limelight, he did not like his older fellow students, and he was not enjoying himself. He may have had the highest IQ of all time. What did he do with all this potential? He wrote a few lesser-known books and became a clerk and factory worker. He disappeared from the spotlight for several decades, until he reemerged in a New York Times "Where Are They Now" article. He was renting a room in a low-income area and working a low-paying job. He sued them for invasion of privacy. Besides a few minor arrests, that is what became of him. So much potential, but in a life of "quiet desperation."

Samson: Hands

Is a gun a tool for liberty or oppression? Is an Opioid a tool for healing or sickness? It depends on who's hands it is in.

After the forgettable judges, the Philistines dominated Israel once again. God wanted to raise up a new deliverer. There was a man named Manoah whose wife was barren. Though they greatly desired a child, no child came. God visited them and assured them she would conceive and that the boy was to be a Nazarite. No razor should touch his head. No wine. No touching dead bodies. He was to be wholly dedicated to the Lord. A year later, the child "Sunny" or Samson was born and the Holy Spirit began to move on him.

Samson developed a relationship with a Philistine from Timnah. In one of his travels to visit her, a lion jumped out of the brush. With the Holy Spirit's help, he tore the lion apart with his bare hands. These hands would be one of the greatest weapons in the whole of scripture. After being betrayed by his fiancé, he had to get some loot to pay a bet she revealed. Then, with his hands, he killed 30 Philistines. While he was gone, she married the best man. When he heard, he burnt down the Philistines' fields by tying torches to the tails of foxes. They retaliated by burning the woman's house down on her. Hostilities escalated. Samson fought them with a "great slaughter." He then escaped to the mountains.

Days later, his tribe came to see him. Were they going to follow him? Would they combine forces and throw off the oppression? Negative. They came to arrest him. Betrayed again. He went with them, and even allowed them to tie him up. After being handed over to the enemy, he snapped the rope like it was yarn. Grabbing the jawbone of a donkey, he laid the smack down on a thousand men and stacked them in heaps. He was so exhausted, and thinking he would die of dehydration, he prayed. God shook the ground and a spring broke out.

You would think after all God did for him, he would turn to God and maybe lead a revival or finish the overthrow of the enemy. Negative. He was sleeping with prostitutes in the city of Gaza. When he heard he was surrounded, he erupted with violence. Grabbing the city gates with his bare hands, he lifted them from the foundation. To make sport of them, he left the gate on a hill.

We next find Samson being seduced by the Philistine Delilah. She had been paid by the five Philistine kings to find the secret of his strength. She teased and teased him. She pressed him, she urged him and "vexed him unto death" until eventually he poured out his whole heart to her. While sleeping on her lap, the Philistine soldiers cut his hair off. He got up to fight like all the times before, but "he did not know the Holy Spirit had left him." Defeated. They gauged out his eyes, chained him up and made him walk around a mill like an ox. His hair began to grow back. On one of their high holy days, they thought to make sport of him in the temple of Dagon. As he entered, he was met with boos and jeers. Rotten fruit and old moldy vegetables were launched at him. "Take me to the middle. Please, place my hands on the center pillars so I can rest," the humbled blind man requested of the servant leading him. Samson leaned on those pillars. He prayed one more time. "God, give me revenge for my eyes. Let me die with these Philistines." He began to push. The Holy Spirit came upon him and the pillars began to shake. Within moments the whole temple collapsed. When the dust settled, Samson's brothers retrieved his body and gave him a proper burial. He killed more Philistines in his death than he had his whole life. He began to deliver Israel.

With his hands, Samson defeated lions, he removed city gates and destroyed a sinful temple.

The devil roams "as a lion seeking whom he may devour." He ought to avoid us. We have Samson power. Life is full of scary surprises. Remember when your brother would hide behind the door just to jump out at you? Or you went into the shed and a mouse ran over your foot? Ahhh! There are scary surprises in life, but we have a greater power. Travelling the road, a lion attacked Samson, and Samson attacked the lion. When he came back through that area, bees had made their home in its carcass. He helped himself to some honey...it was a sweet victory.

With his hands, Samson removed city gates. It reminds us that "the gates of Hell will not stand against us." We raid. By God's power, not ours, lost souls will be found. Our aggressive style to preach the gospel, write books, start churches, send missionaries, knock on doors, and host events are all Hell-storming efforts. When the gate is removed, people can leave.

Samson with his hands destroyed their sinful temple. "We tear down every thought that is against God." We live in enemy territory. The god of this age has blinded many, but we have the power of God. The way we used to think and the way we think now are very different. In seeing the error of our ways, we repented.

There lived a wise old man in a small farm town. For decades, he had loved his town. He was a teacher for many years and volunteered for every sport at the community center. Those days were behind him. In the evenings, he would sit in his rocking chair and listen to his birds. Some of the local rebellious youth were tired of hearing about how wise he was and what an example he was. Before the old man came outside, they ran onto his porch. The ringleader opened the bird cage and squeezed the poor bird. Hearing the commotion, the old man came outside. His eyes were weak. "Hey, old fool. I have heard you are wise, but I don't believe it. I got your bird behind my back. Prove how wise you are. One question: 'Is your bird alive or dead?'" The boy thought if he said "alive," he would squeeze it to death that instant. If he said "dead," he would throw it in his face alive. He thought it would be a lose-lose scenario for the old man. But the wise man was wise. He had the perfect answer. "If my bird is alive or dead….well….I suppose that is completely in your hands."

Samson: Unexpected Weapons

General Hannible was notorious for creativity on the battlefield. In a naval battle against King Eumenes II in 190 BC, he catapulted jars of poisonous snakes to their ships. The dread, the bites, and the chaos led to a Hannibal victory.

Archimedes was another creative military mind. "The Claw" was a massive beam with a hand-like end to batter incoming ships. He also implemented a huge magnifying glass to lazar sunbeam opposing sails.

In recounting the story of Samson, think of all the wild ideas. He used 300 jackals, the jawbone of a donkey and pillars in a temple. We, too, are called to be creative in our tools to advance the gospel.

Genghis Khan once enlisted a thousand cats. He was sieging the city of Volohai. The fortifications would lead to a long, draining, unsustainable stalemate. Genghis offered bizarre peace terms. "If you will give me a thousand cats and a thousand birds as a tribute to our god, we can leave you alone." Although they thought it strange, they were more excited to get rid of the enemy army. Once they brought the animals out the front gate, Genghis' men had torches tied to ropes which they quickly fastened to the cats. Once lit, they hopped back over the fence and ran amuck spreading fire and chaos everywhere. Samson did something like this with 300 jackals on the Philistine fields.

Ask yourself "What is plentiful?" Use what is close by. What is already in motion? For example, people who love sports are already playing them. Our church puts on leagues and tournaments. We don't have to teach people how to play, we simply receive the mass amounts of players looking for a place to hoop. Christians are natural coaches. We teach. We observe. We listen. We love people. Opening up sports ministry is a bit like catching those wild jackals and letting them loose.

Samson is clever. "Heaps upon heaps, I have piled them with the jawbone of a donkey." It is a play on words. In Hebrew, "heaps" and "donkey" are almost the same word. Samson finds a way to win. Even though he is terribly unfaithful, going after prostitutes and seeking revenge, he has faith. He knows God hears him. When we realize God wants to answer our prayers, we will pray even more. Samson leaves the whorehouse, and minutes later there is a miracle. It was not because of him; it was in spite of him that God showed His power.

There is an old way. It is a way of traditions, expectations, and the way people are taught. The natural man needs structure.

Some of these ways are opposed to God. We often call people "good" because they are compared to our old ways. The old ways are like pillars. We lean on them. We are comforted by them. They give us rest and security. But those old ways must be destroyed. Only God is good. Our comfort can be our downfall. When it falls apart, what is left?

Samson dies in enemy territory, but is given an honorable burial. He reminds us of Christ. Both had a supernatural birth. Both had a sacrificial death. Both had a proper burial. But Jesus had a powerful resurrection!

A mom was very faithful in bringing her daughter to church. She longed for her husband to come. She prayed and prayed. In NFL season, Sundays were for football. Then, one day after church, the little girl brought her dad a gift. It was a picture of her family in a popsicle-stick frame. At the top was a crayon drawing of a colored cross. "Daddy, Daddy, I know you love us and I wanted to give you this. I made it for you. And daddy, as much as you love us, Jesus loves us even more! He died for us, that is why I put the cross on it!" The dad was so moved, and felt the presence of God. He began going to church the next Sunday and never looked back. Out of all the things to win a heart, it was a popsicle-stick framed picture with a child's message of good news.

Eli: Internal Disaster

A lucky rabbit's foot, a lucky penny, or a relative's old cross neckless, do any really help you?

After the story of Samson, we come to Eli the high priest. He respected his sons more than God. His boys were corrupt. They extorted the worshipers, stole from the tabernacle and fornicated. Eli knew, but did nothing. God was going to replace this family from serving and raise up a priest after His heart, a boy who had been committed by his mother to serve. Samuel was hearing from God while they were satisfying their sinful desires. God had spoken to Samuel about how Eli's house would be judged. They would all die in one day. He even told his adoptive father. Samuel was different; he feared God.

When the Philistines came to attack, Eli's sons, Hophni and Phinehas brought the ark of the Covenant to the army camp. The troops were so roused, they cheered and the earth shook. Hearing their excitement, the Philistines gave a great speech. The battle ensued. Israel was defeated. Phinehas and Hophni were killed. The Ark was captured. When news reached Eli, he had a heart attack, fell backward from his seat, broke his neck and died. This was a disaster. Phinehas' wife went into labor and named the child "Ichabod," meaning "the glory has departed." That day ended 20 years of Eli judging the nation.

Internal disasters ensue when we fear opinions over the Omnipotent; when we forsake God's favor. This will cause whole families to suffer.

It is sad when a teenager is peer-pressured into a crime. They steal something they don't like, they stomp on a kid they don't know, or they shout mean things they don't believe. When we fear foolish people more than we fear God, that is a problem. Eli was like that. He cared more about what his boys thought about him than he cared for the approval of God. He wanted to be their friend more than a national leader. He insulted God by not correcting them. It is like an evil, bribable judge who keeps releasing serious criminals. God sees that dereliction and will punish it. How would you feel about a police officer who never arrested anyone? To ignore your obligations is an evil. Eli allowed wickedness.

Do you have God's favor? Do you want God's favor? If you had it, would you keep it? Eli forsook it. When the boy Samuel prophesied that he and his sons would die in one day, Eli expected it to happen. He did not repent. He did not change his ways to try and mitigate it. He waited. Not even wicked King Ahab just accepted his sentence; he had moments of repentance. The Bible says of Esau that he "looked for a place to repent" he wanted to change. Once he realized what he lost, he looked for a way to get it back.

A pastor was in his last season of decades of church ministry. For years he looked forward to his retirement on a small farm just about an hour out of town. He finally purchased the property and began fixing it up. He was faithful to serve his congregation and on his days off he was working on the farm. New fences, paint on the barn, the fields re-tilled, re-planted and animals brought in, it was a joy for him. As often as he could, he would dash out there and put in some work. "Pastor, I passed your farm the other day. Wow! It looks great! You and the Lord must be doing some seriously good work!" Without thinking, the minister responded: "You should have seen it when the Lord had it all to Himself." God expects us to work. He is not our rabbit's foot or lucky penny.

Samuel: Asked

The greatest quarterback in NFL history was once a replacement. Tom Brady was fourth string in his rookie year with one appearance, throwing three passes for a grand total of six yards. By his second season he would be second string. When Drew Brees got hurt, Brady filled in and never looked back. He would go on to win seven Super Bowls.

Hannah was barren. Maybe worse than that, her husband's other wife, Peninnah, was having babies left and right. She was a mean girl about it too. Hannah was so desperate she would pray so hard and no words would come out. At the tabernacle, Eli rebuked her for being drunk. "I am not drunk, just desperate for a child." She told the Lord if she conceived, she would give the child to the Lord. God answered. Samuel, whose name means "asked for" was born. She treasured the time they had. After he was weaned, he was brought to the tabernacle to serve. That would be his life.

While Eli's sons were so corrupt, Samuel kept serving the Lord. He cut the wood and washed the utensils. He swept the ashes and cleaned the dishes. All the menial tasks were his.

God was with him. Not one of his words fell to the ground. What Samuel said, happened. In those days there was no widespread revelation of God's word, but Samuel had it. When Eli and his sons died, the mantle of leadership would fall to him. He set up a circuit of teaching God's word and giving judgements. The people loved him and received him. After the Philistines recovered from Samson's devastation, they regrouped and sent their army into Israel's territory. "Samuel, Samuel, what will we do?" Panic spread. "We will pray," he declared. And pray he did. God sent a thunderstorm to scare the enemy. They turned on each other and a mighty victory was given to Israel.

The years passed and the people did not want Samuel's sons to lead. They were not like him. They were unjust and bribable. "Give us a king. We want to be like other nations," they demanded. Samuel felt so rejected. "They are not rejecting you, but they are rejecting Me. Give them a king. Give them one after their own heart," the Lord answered. Saul would be anointed twice by Samuel; once in private and once before the nation. Samuel was the last of the judges because he led the nation into the monarchy.

Like Samuel, you have been asked for. God answers you. You are someone's answer.

One knee down. A ring in the hand. A tear in the eye. It's the proposal. He is asking for you.

Hannah asked and asked and asked for a son. Samuel was so, so, so loved before he was born. When she conceived, she was so excited. It was supernatural. God heard her. She would be faithful to keep her word and give the child back to the Lord. God would bless her with five more kids.

It has been well said that "God always answers. He answers with 'yes' or 'no' or 'not yet.'" Samuel was always asking God. He was many things: a judge, a prophet, a priest, a father, a husband and a teacher, but most of all he was a prayer warrior! "I will not sin by ceasing to pray for you," he declared to the nation. Thunder rang out at his beckon. Kings knelt before him to receive oil. God used him mightily.

You are being waited for. Singles who want a godly spouse, I believe they are out there. They are the answer to your prayer and you are the answer to their prayer. Stay prepared to serve. Samuel did not make excuses. He didn't say, "my parents left me" or "I was raised around hypocrites." He kept shoveling. Kept cleaning. And kept praying.

Anthony Johnson was an undefeated heavyweight champion. He held the WBA, IBF, WBO, and IBO heavyweight titles. With a record of 22-0, with 21 of those by knockout, he was to be feared. In 2012 he received an Olympic Gold. He looked like a super hero with bigger muscles. He was scheduled to fight Jarrell Miller, but Miller failed several drug tests. A last-minute replacement was needed. Enter Andy Ruiz, Jr., looking like the Michelin Man's real-life brother. Johnson was the -2500 favorite. Ruiz was a +1200 dog. If you bet $100 on Ruiz, you would have won $1200. Four times in the fight, Ruiz battered Johnson to the mat. In the seventh round, Ruiz put the beating on Johnson to the point of referee stoppage. An unexpected replacement became the champion.

Conclusion

God calls us to be His soldiers. He has equipped us with His armor. Jesus came on a military campaign to "Destroy the works of the devil." Jesus trained 12 disciples to continue the advancement of His Kingdom. Before the resurrection, Judas would be taken by Satan. Peter would suffer cowardly setbacks. But this was not a fragile squadron. Matthias would replace Judas with a quick roll of the dice. Peter would recover and lead with a new vision. Power came from on high. Each believer was filled to become a witness. Daily our numbers grow. Each one comes at the expense of our adversary. We are here to advance. We are still alive so we can advance the Kingdom. You are not called to retreat. Go forward, soldier.

We live in enemy territory. But our mindset and culture are that of Heaven, not of earth. Our commanding officer was murdered in the ugliest way. Without quarter. Without mercy. Unjustly they tortured Him, objectified Him and hung Him on a cross high, for all to see. But He didn't stay dead, He rose. The power that raised Him now dwells in us. The purpose of the sacrifice is that we could be saved.

That armor is required. Looking at the judges, we see those who fought the good fight and those who didn't. We see the divine creativity and incredible victories, and the tragic and unnecessary defeats.

God has a special suit of armor for you. Will you wear it? Will you use it? Will you walk in victory?

www.ingramcontent.com/pod-product-compliance
Lightning Source LLC
Chambersburg PA
CBHW060417050426
42449CB00009B/1996